Roses, Laughter & Lullabies

18 Classical Songs for Mezzo-Soprano
Ages Mid-Teens and Up

T0081972

Compiled by Joan Frey Boytim

To access companion recorded piano accompaniments online, visit:
www.halleonard.com/mylibrary

4687-0168-0237-5226

ISBN 978-1-4234-3953-0

HAL•LEONARD®
CORPORATION
7777 W. BLUEMOUND RD. P.O. BOX 13819 MILWAUKEE, WI 53213

In Australia Contact:
Hal Leonard Australia Pty. Ltd.
4 Lentara Court
Cheltenham, Victoria, 3192 Australia
Email: ausadmin@halleonard.com.au

Visit Hal Leonard Online at
www.halleonard.com

PREFACE

Roses, Laughter & Lullabies is a supplementary classical solo book compiled for musically secure late middle and senior high school mezzo-sopranos and altos, or for adult students. Included are accompaniments, recorded by Laura Ward, for practice for those who use these learning aids.

This volume contains 18 songs to complement *The First Book of Mezzo-Soprano/Alto Solos, Parts I, II,* and *III.* Even though there are several easy songs such as "Cradle Song," "Birds in the Night," and "The Winds Are Calling," most of the songs explore a different genre of song not often found in mezzo-soprano teaching material due to style, length, and flexibility demands. There are a number of selections that were definitely too long to include in the "First Book Series," but fit very easily within this anthology. Some of the pieces have been out of print and many are probably unknown to many teachers.

Many mezzo-sopranos who reach a certain level of musical maturity love to sing florid songs; therefore, you will find melismatic pieces such as "Should He Upbraid," "O, Bid Your Faithful Ariel Fly," a different setting of "Under the Greenwood Tree," and "Spring Comes Laughing." Several songs have very dramatic qualities, including "Hymn to the Night," "Two Roses," and "Tears." As a result, the ranges of some of these pieces are somewhat wider than usual. Within the book, the musical level spans from easy to moderately difficult and the accompaniments vary from simple to complex. I believe these songs will provide teachers with new opportunities to expand the repertoire usually sung by student mezzo-sopranos and altos. This volume will suit many adult students as well as the mature teenager.

Joan Frey Boytim
May, 2008

CONTENTS

The price of this publication includes access to companion recorded piano accompaniments online, for download or streaming, using the unique code found on the title page. Visit **www.halleonard.com/mylibrary** and enter the access code.

BIRDS IN THE NIGHT
(A Lullaby)

Lionel H. Lewin

Arthur Sullivan

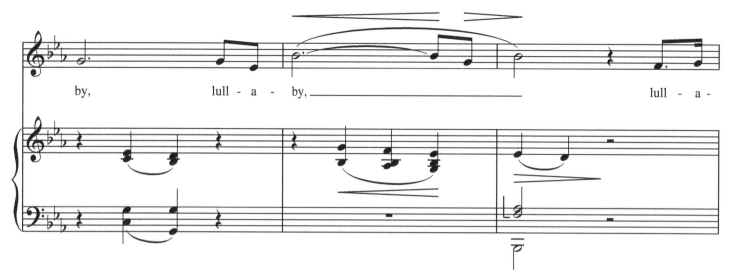

by,   lull - a - by,_____   lull - a -

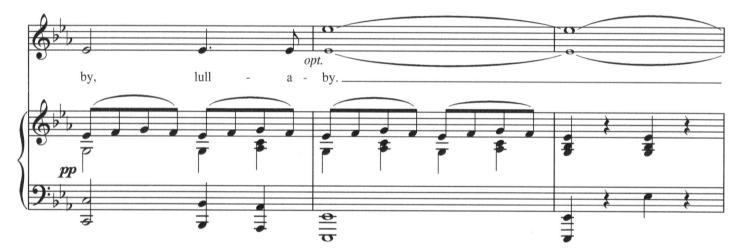

by,   lull - a - by._____

Life __ may be sad __ for __ us __ that __ wake,

Sleep, lit - tle bird, and dream not why, Soon __ is the sleep __ but

God __ can __ break, When an - gels __ whis - per, whis - per, an - gels whis - per __

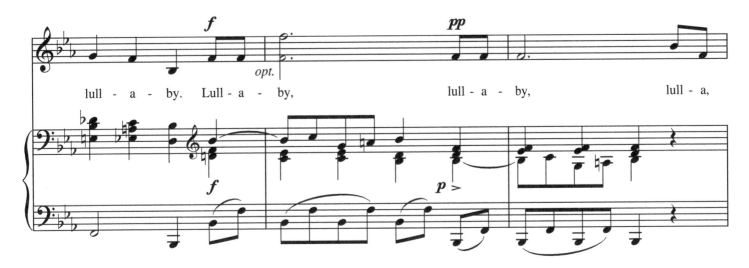

lull - a - by. Lull - a - by, lull - a - by, lull - a,

lull - a, lull - a, lull - a, lull - a - by, Lull - a - by, __ ba - by,

while the hours — run, Fair — may the day be, When — night is done,

Lull - a - by, ba - by, while the hours run, Lull - a - by, lull - a -

by, lull - a - by, _____ lull - a -

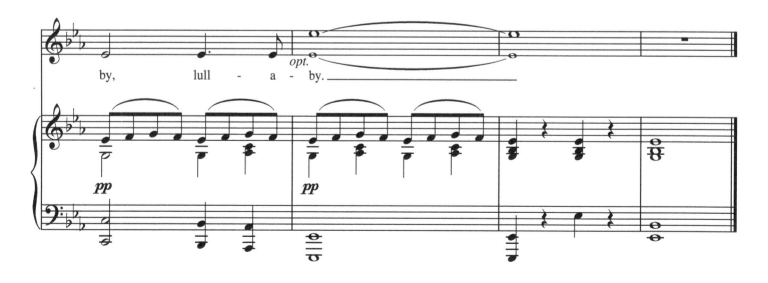

by, lull - a - by. _____

CRADLE SONG

English words by M.X. Hayes

Franz Schubert

Slum - ber, slum - ber, in sweet dreams_ re - pos - ing, While pro - tects _____ thee thy fond moth - er's _ arm; All her rich - es, here _____ en - clos - ing Holds she in _____ her clasp so true _ and _ warm.

pp

Slum - ber, slum - ber,

on thy down - y __ pil - low, Love's hymn round __ thee mu - sic sweet __ shall __ make;

And a lil - y and __ a rose - bud Shall re - ward __ thee

when thou dost __ a - wake.

THE FORSAKEN MAID

Thomas Smart

H. Lane Wilson

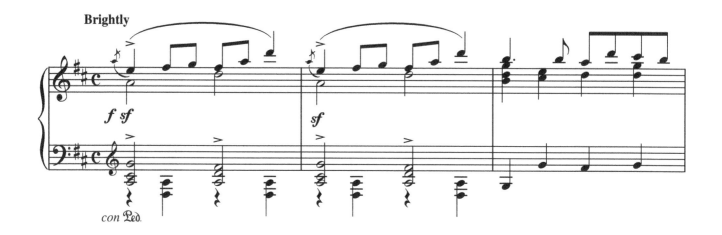

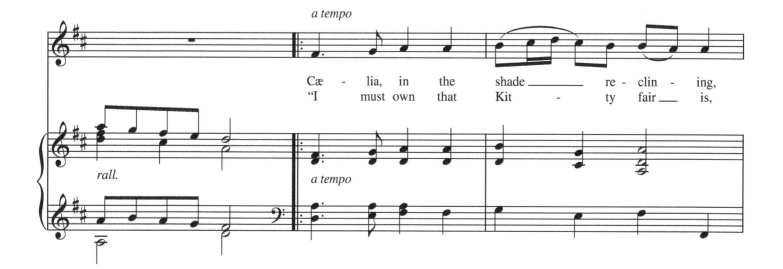

Cæ - lia, in the shade _____ re - clin - ing,
"I must own that Kit - ty fair _____ is,

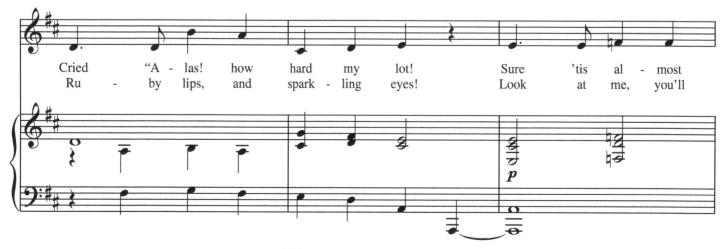

Cried "A - las! how hard my lot! Sure 'tis al - most
Ru - by lips, and spark - ling eyes! Look at me, you'll

past de - clin - ing, That I thus should be for - got.
think that there is Charm that might a heart sur - prise;

Co - lin fond - ly
Art - ful Chlo - e,

sighs for Kit - ty; Chlo - e is young Da - mon's flame!
each be - guil - ing, Beau - ty has not more than me!

Kiss - ing, court - ing, all so pret - ty,
Tho' to all she's al - ways smil - ing,

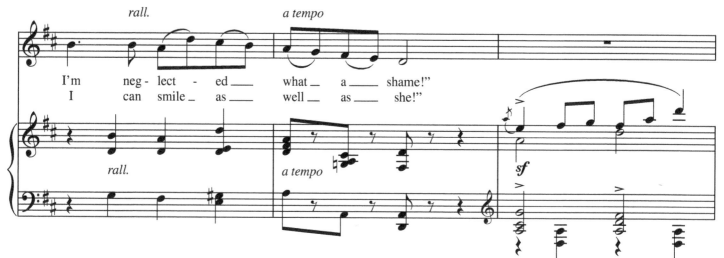

I'm neg - lect - ed __ what __ a __ shame!"
I can smile __ as __ well __ as __ she!"

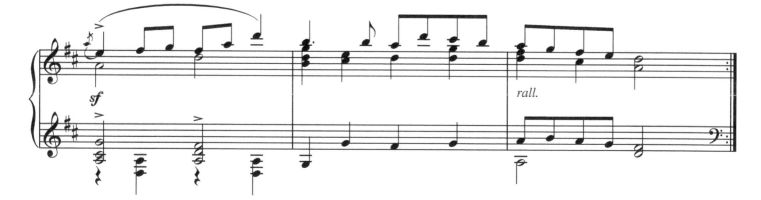

Youth - ful Stre - phon, o - ver - hear - ing, Was re - solved to

take her part; To the fair one soon ap - pear - ing,

Kind - ly sooth'd her _ ach - ing heart.

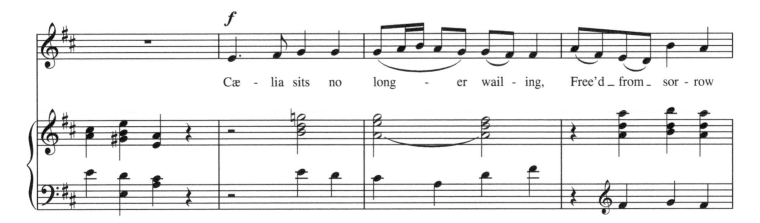

f

Cæ - lia sits no long - er wail - ing, Free'd _ from _ sor - row

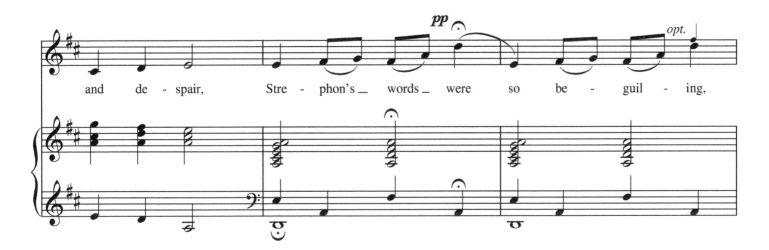

pp *opt.*

and de - spair, Stre - phon's _ words _ were so be - guil - ing,

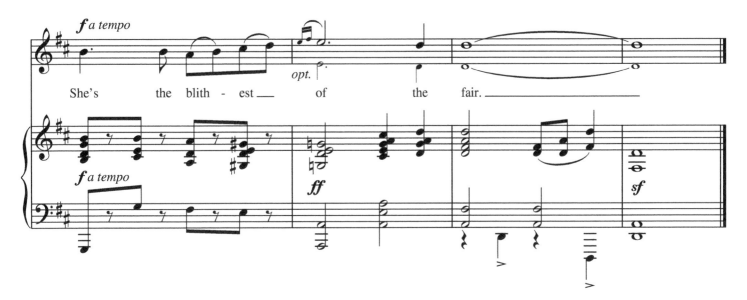

f a tempo

She's the blith - est _ of the fair. _

opt. *ff* *f a tempo* *sf*

I HAVE TWELVE OXEN

John Ireland

17

lit - tle pret - ty boy?

I have twelve ox - en, they be fair and white, And they go a - graz - ing

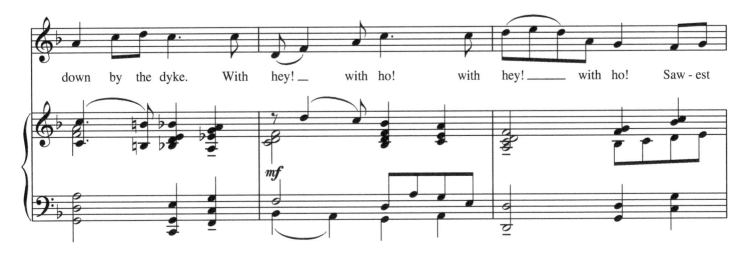

down by the dyke. With hey! __ with ho! with hey! ___ with ho! Saw - est

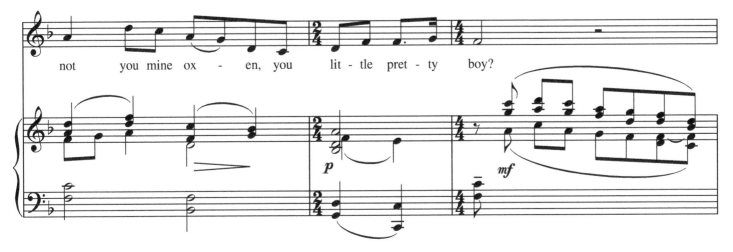

not you mine ox - en, you lit - tle pret - ty boy?

I have twelve ox - en, they be fair and black, And

they go a - graz - ing down by the lake. With hey! _ with ho! with

cresc.

hey! _____ with ho! Saw - est not you mine ox - en, you lit - tle pret - ty

poco meno mosso

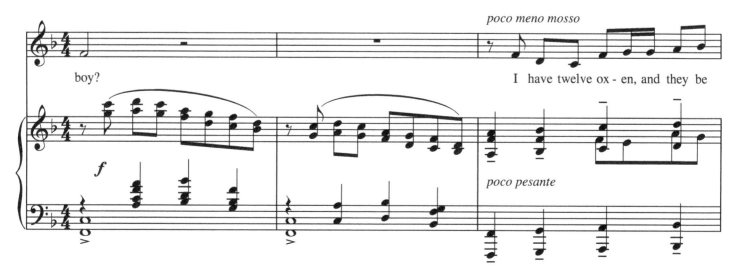

boy?

I have twelve ox - en, and they be

poco pesante

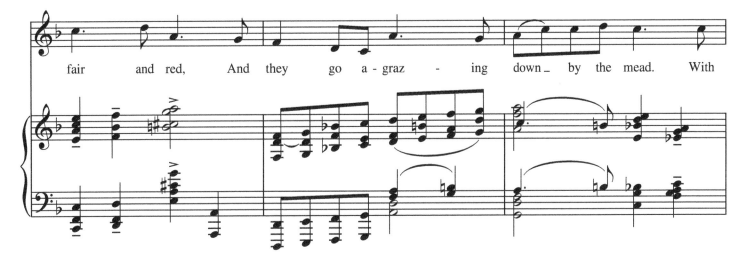

fair and red, And they go a-graz - ing down by the mead. With

a tempo

hey! _ with ho! with hey! _____ with ho! Saw-est not you mine ox - en, you

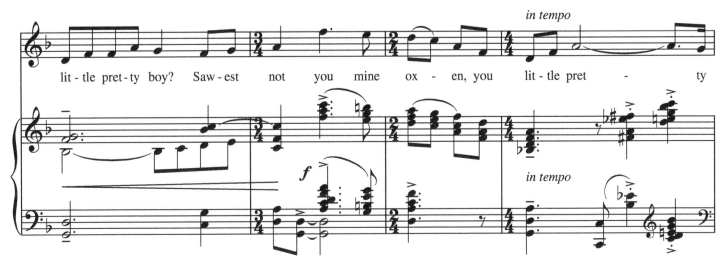

lit - tle pret-ty boy? Saw-est not you mine ox - en, you lit - tle pret - ty

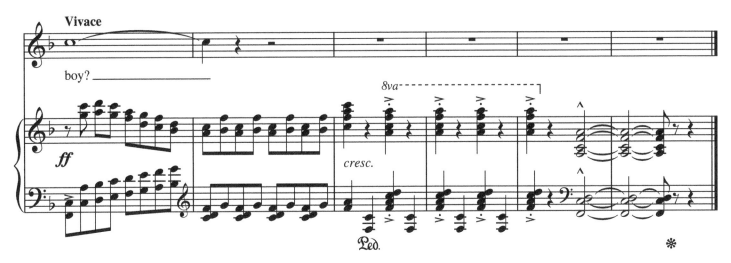

Vivace

boy? _____

HYMN TO THE NIGHT

Henry Wadsworth Longfellow

Lewis Campbell-Tipton

Sweep through her mar - ble

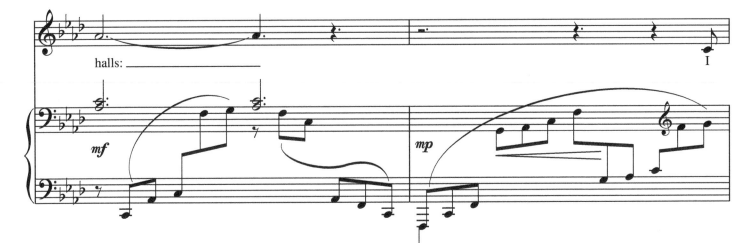

halls: _____ I

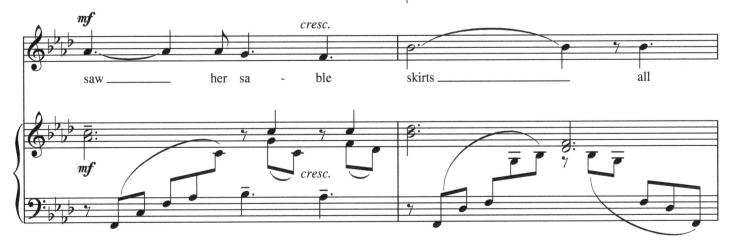

saw _____ her sa - ble skirts _____ all

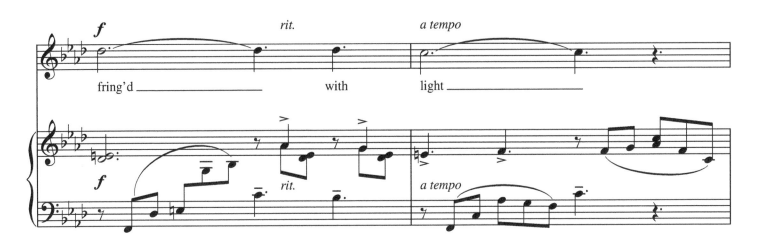

fring'd _____ with light _____

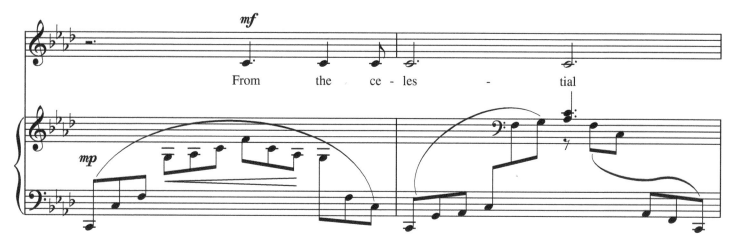

From the ce - les - tial walls.

walls. I felt her pres - ence, by its

spell of might, Stoop o'er me from a -

bove; the calm, ma - jes - tic pres - ence of the night, As

of _____ the one I love.

In moderate movement

O ho - ly night! _____ from thee I learn to

bear _____ What man has borne be - fore! _____

24

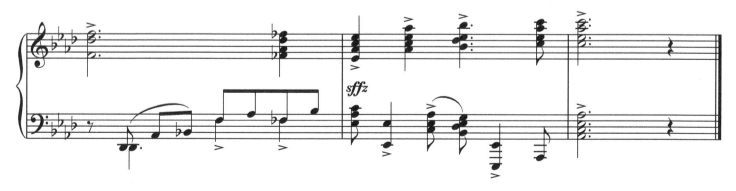

I WILL GO WITH
MY FATHER A-PLOUGHING

Joseph Campbell

Roger Quilter

26

sing to the pa-tient hors-es With the lark in the shine of the

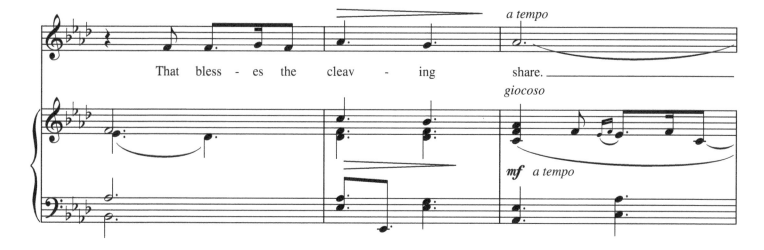

air, _____ And my fa-ther will sing the plough-song _____

That bless-es the cleav-ing share. _____

_____ I will go with my fa-ther a-sow-ing _____ To the

red field by ___ the sea, And the rooks and the gulls and the

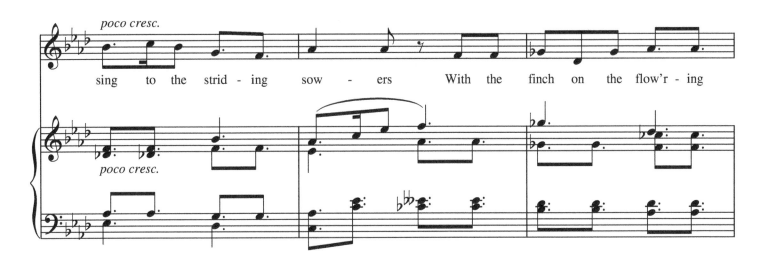

star - lings Will come flock - ing af - ter me. I will

sing to the strid - ing sow - ers With the finch on the flow'r - ing

sloe, And my fa - ther will sing the seed - song ___

That on - ly the wise men know. _____ I will

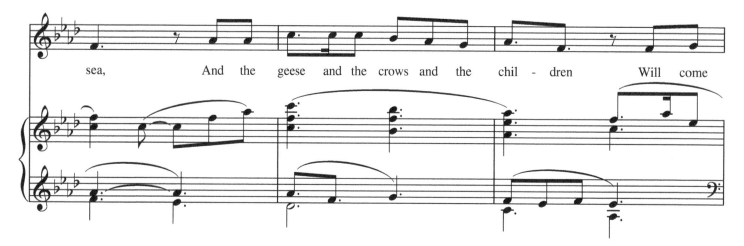

go with my fa - ther a - reap - ing To the brown field by the

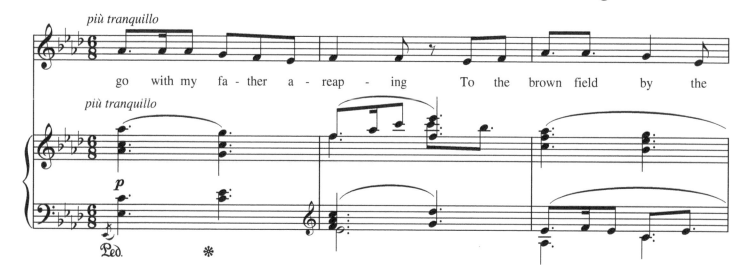

sea, And the geese and the crows and the chil - dren Will come

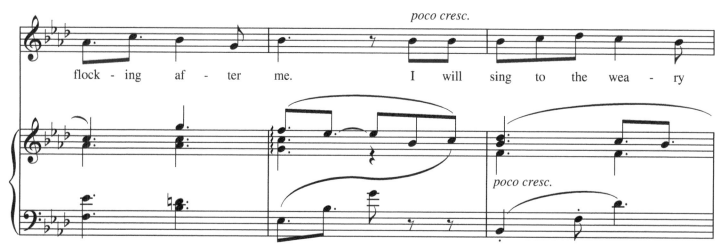

flock - ing af - ter me. I will sing to the wea - ry

IT WAS A LOVER AND HIS LASS

William Shakespeare

Henry Clough-Leighter

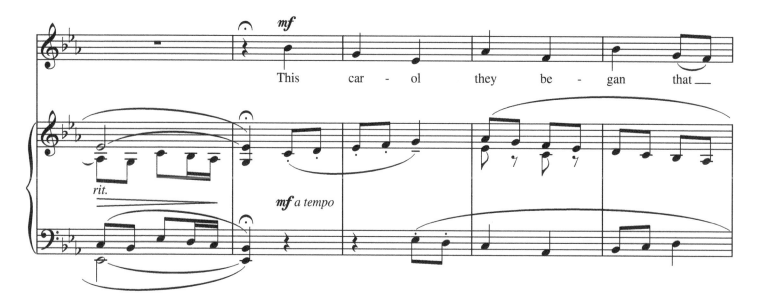

This car - ol they be - gan that

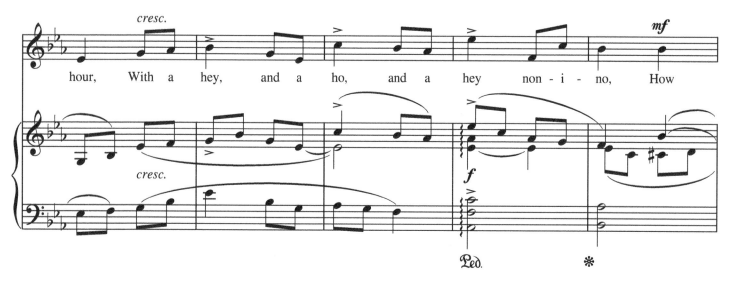

hour, With a hey, and a ho, and a hey non - i - no, How

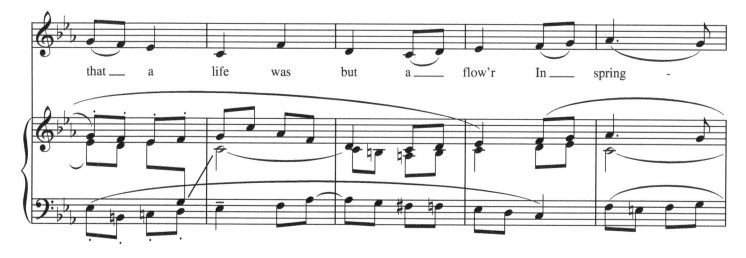

that a life was but a flow'r In spring -

JEANNETTE AND HER LITTLE WOODEN SHOES

Robert B. Smith

Victor Herbert

Allegretto molto moderato

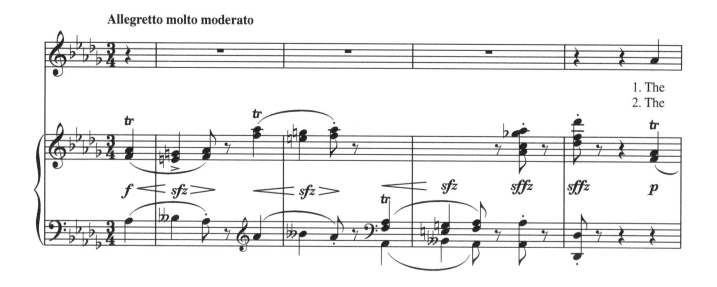

1. The
2. The

live - ly Jean - nette, Far famed for fri - vol - i - ty, A
King's son and heir Found her quite a - dor - a - ble, Pa

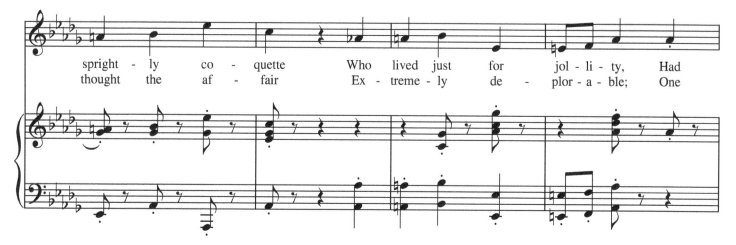

spright - ly co - quette Who lived just for jol - li - ty, Had
thought the af - fair Ex - treme - ly de - plor - a - ble; One

plen - ty of suit - ors, had on - ly to choose: And
cold win - ter night, when the town was a - sleep, The

be - ing a Dutch girl, she wore wood - en shoes. __ When she
two stole a - way, though the snow was quite deep. __ The

stole out at night all the town knew the news, When they
King cried: "Pur - sue them! Which way did they go?" The

heard the pit - pat - ter of her wood - en shoes. __ Then the
guards and the court - iers they ran to and fro; ___ And he

lads, half a - sleep, oh how jeal - ous they'd get, And they'd
might be pur - su - ing those two lov - ers yet, But

poco rit.

say to them - selves, "Who is out with Jean - nette?"
those wood - en shoe - tracks in the snow spell'd Jean - nette!

sfz *a tempo* *sfz*

Clip clop clop! Clip clop clop! O - ver the tiles. Her
Clip clop clop! Clip clop clop! There in the snow Her

feet were pe - tite, But you heard her for miles, ___ With her
feet so pe - tite, Showed them which way to go, ___ With her

LOVE IS A SICKNESS FULL OF WOES

Samuel Daniel

Horatio Parker

Love is a sick - ness full _____ of woes, All rem - e - dies re - fus - ing; A plant ___ that most ___ with cut - ting

grows, Most bar - ren with best us - ing, Why

so?_____ Why so?_____ More we en -

joy it, more it dies; If not en - joy'd it

sigh - ing cries, Heigh - ho!_____ Heigh - ho!_____

Heigh - ho!

Love is a tor - ment

of ___ the mind, A tem - pest ev - er - last -

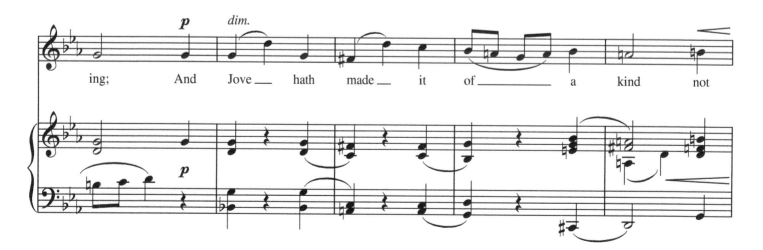

ing; And Jove ___ hath made ___ it of ___ a kind not

well, _ nor full, nor fast - ing, Why so? _____ Why

so? _____ More we en - joy it, more it dies;

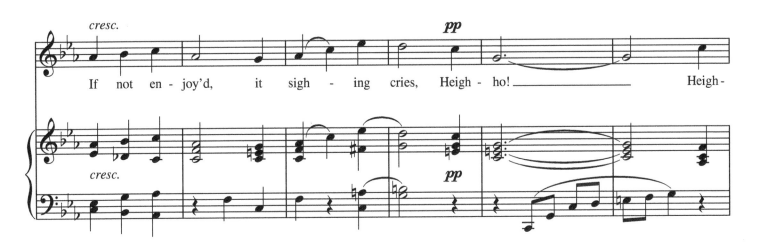

If not en - joy'd, it sigh - ing cries, Heigh - ho! _____ Heigh-

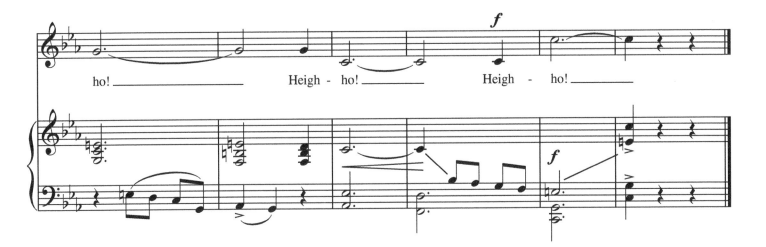

ho! _____ Heigh - ho! _____ Heigh - ho! _____

O, BID YOUR FAITHFUL ARIEL FLY

William Shakespeare

Thomas Linley

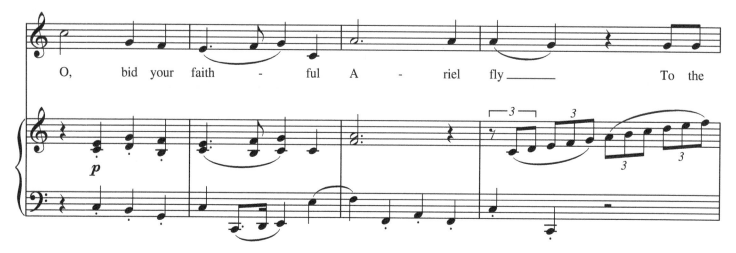

O, bid your faith - ful A - riel fly _____ To the

far - - - - - thest In - dian sky! And

then at thy a - fresh com -

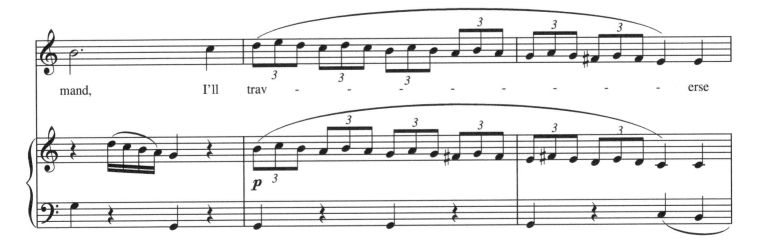

mand, I'll trav - - - - - - - erse

o'er _____ the sil - ver _

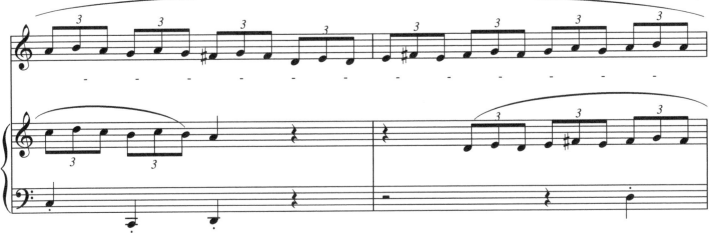

tals nev - - - - -

er   sleep.   O,   bid your

faith - ful A - riel fly_____ To the far - -

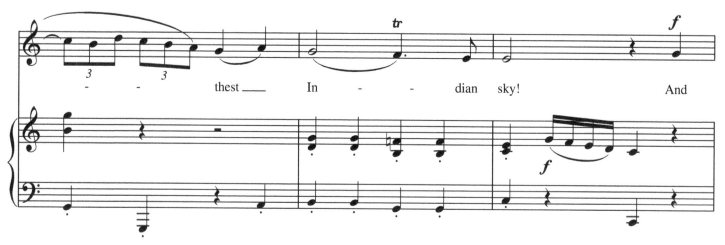

thest __ In - - dian sky! And

then, at __ thy a - fresh com -

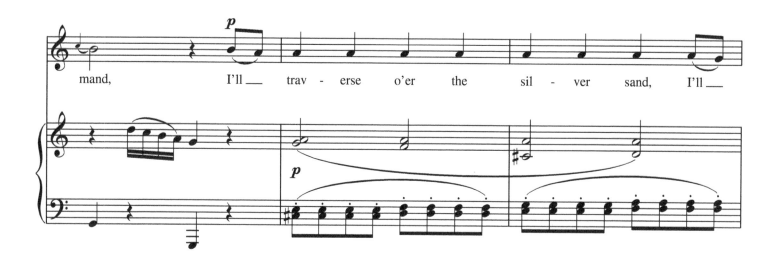

mand, I'll __ trav - erse o'er the sil - ver sand, I'll __

trav - erse o'er the sil - ver sand. I'll climb the moun - tains,

plunge the deep, I'll climb the moun - tains,

plunge the deep, I, like mor - tals, nev - er sleep,

I, like mor - tals, nev - er sleep, I, like mor - -

48

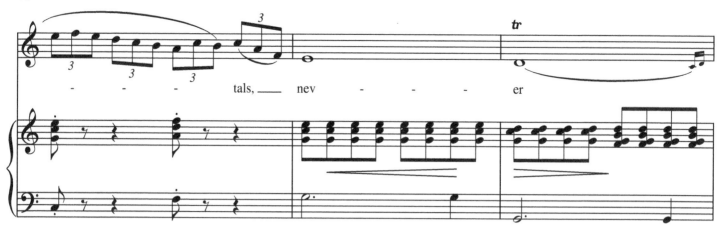

tals, ___ nev - - - er

sleep.

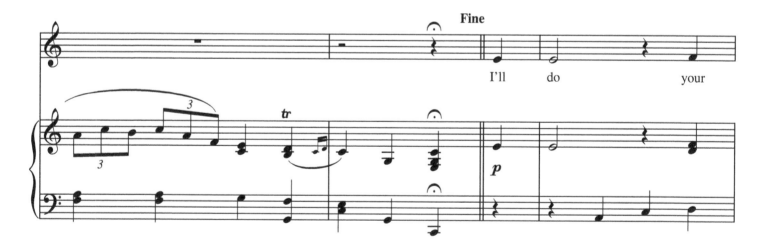

Fine

I'll do your

task, ___ what - e'er ___ it ___ be, ___ Not with ill

will, but mer - ri - ly, mer - ri - ly, mer - ri - ly; what - e'er it

be, Not with ill will, __ but mer - ri - ly,

mer - ri - ly, mer - ri - ly, mer - ri - ly,

Not __ with _ ill __ will, __ but mer - - ri - ly.

a piacere

colla voce

D.S. al Fine

SHOULD HE UPBRAID

William Shakespeare

Henry Rowley Bishop

Moderato ma brillante

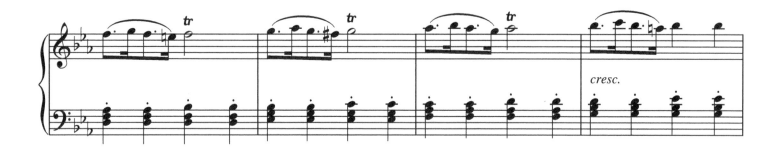

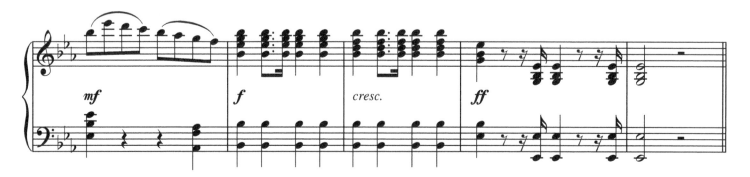

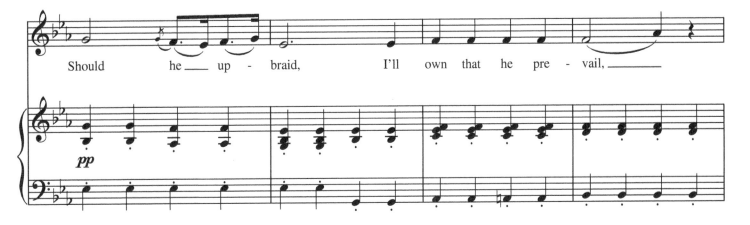

Should he — up - braid, I'll own that he pre - vail, —

And sing as — sweet - ly as the night - in - gale; —

Say that — he — frown, I'll say his looks I view —

As morn - ing ro - ses — new - ly — tipped with

52

ro - ses tipped with dew, _____ _____

As _____ ro - ses ___ tipped with dew, _____

tipped with dew, As morn - ing ro - ses

tipped with dew.

cresc. **f** *cresc.* **ff**

Say he be mute, I'll an - swer with a smile,

And dance and play, and ___ wrin - kled care be - guile,

And dance and play, ___ dance ___ and play, and

wrin - kled care beguile.

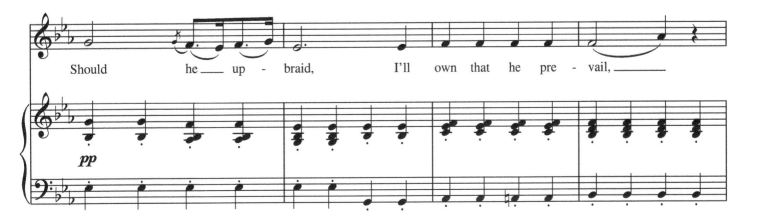

Should he up - braid, I'll own that he pre - vail, _____

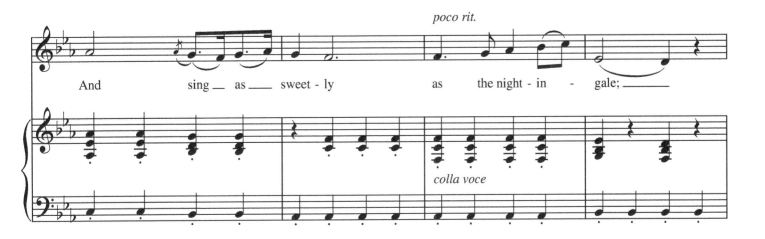

And sing as sweet - ly as the night - in - gale; _____

Say that __ he __ frown, I'll say his looks I view __

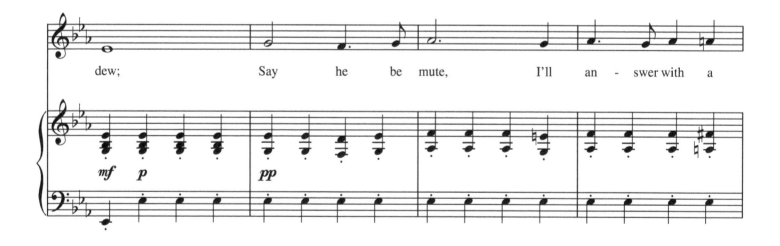

As morn - ing ro - ses __ new - ly __ tipped with

dew; Say he be mute, I'll an - swer with a

smile, And dance __ and play, __ and dance __ and

play, dance ____ and play, dance ____ and

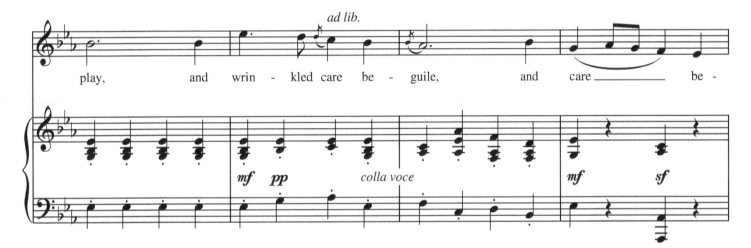

ad lib.

play, and wrin - kled care be - guile, and care ____ be -

mf *pp* *colla voce* *mf* *sf*

guile, I'll dance, ____ play, ____

sf *pp*

dance, ____ play, ____ dance ____ and

cresc.

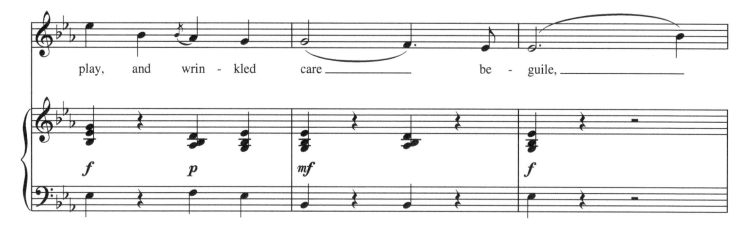

play, and wrin - kled care _____ be - guile, _____

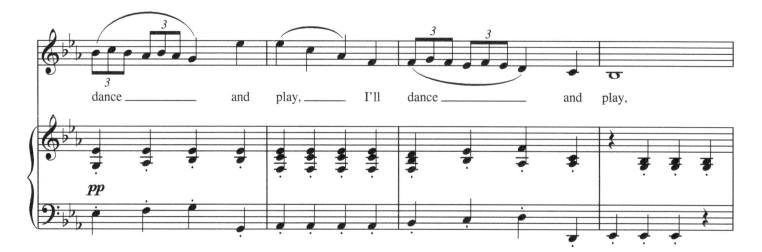

dance _____ and play, _____ I'll dance _____ and play,

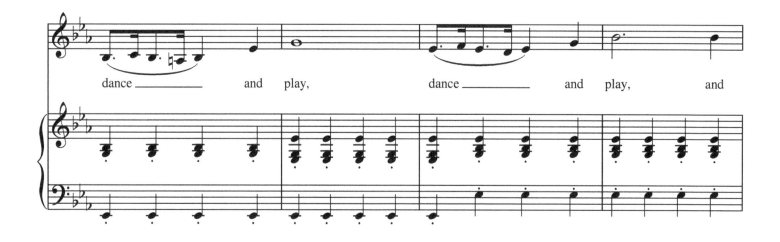

dance _____ and play, dance _____ and play, and

wrin - kled care be - guile, and care _____ be - guile, I'll

dance, _____ play, _____ dance, _____

play, _____ dance _____ and play, and wrin - kled

care _____ be - guile.

SPRING COMES LAUGHING

Dena Tempest

Molly Carew

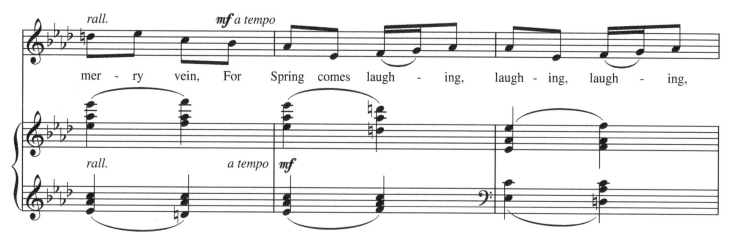

mer - ry vein, For Spring comes laugh - ing, laugh - ing, laugh - ing,

laugh - ing __ o'er _____ the hills!

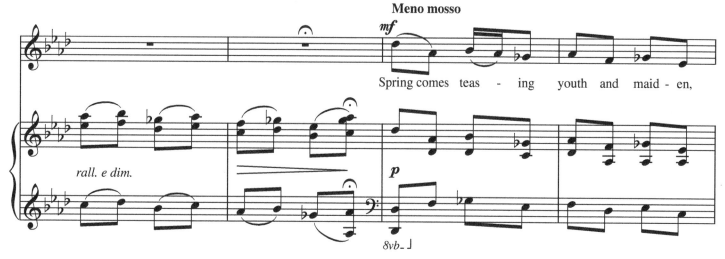

Spring comes teas - ing youth and maid - en,

Spring! with her woo - ing song! ____ Whis - pers to lov - ers, brave and fair,

who shall de - ny that day is fair When Spring _____ comes

laugh - ing, _ laugh - ing o'er the hills! Comes laugh - ing, laugh - ing, laugh - ing,

laugh - ing, laugh - ing, laugh - ing o'er _____ the hills!

TWO ROSES

Emily Selinger

Hallett Gilberté

low _____ winds that sigh _____ winds that blow, _____ There
low _____ winds that sigh _____ winds that blow, _____ But the

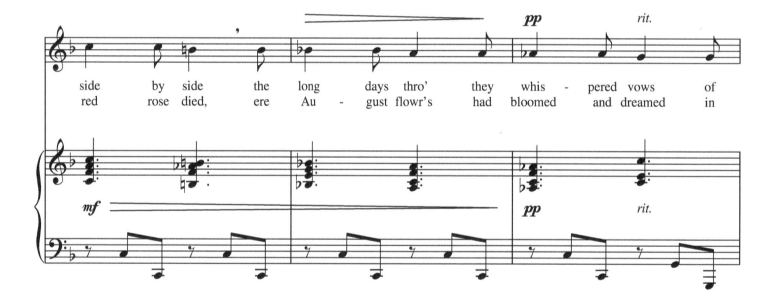

side by side the long days thro' they whis - pered vows of
red rose died, ere Au - gust flowr's had bloomed and dreamed in

love so true, By sun and moon, by ___ shine and dew, } Sing
gar - den bowers, and the white rose pined, till ___ Au - tumn hours, }

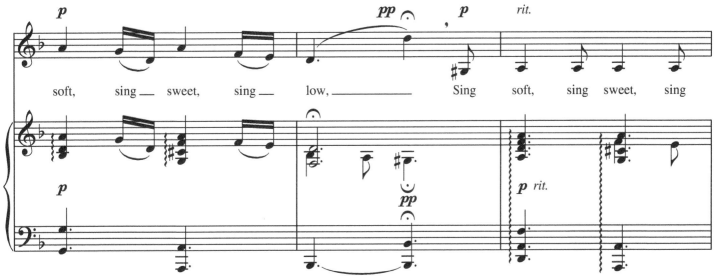

soft, sing — sweet, sing — low, _____ Sing soft, sing sweet, sing

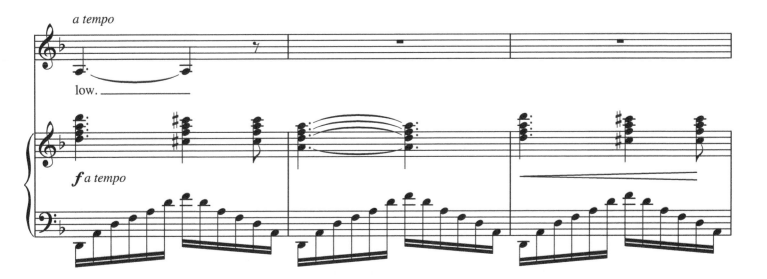

low. _____

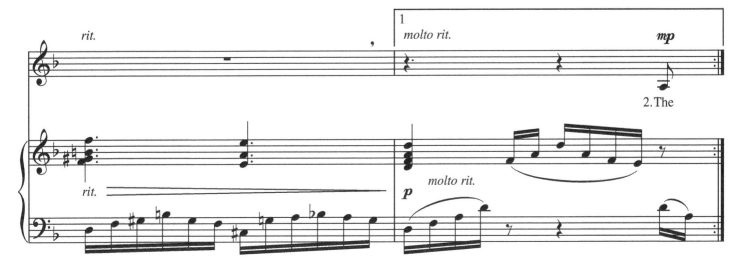

2. The

68

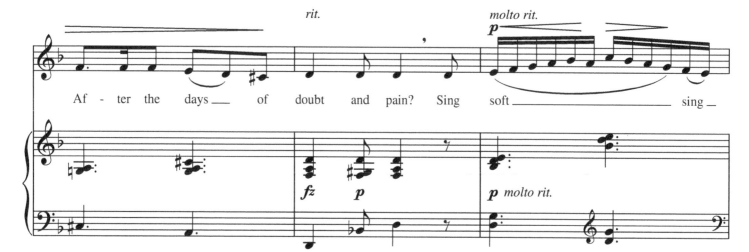

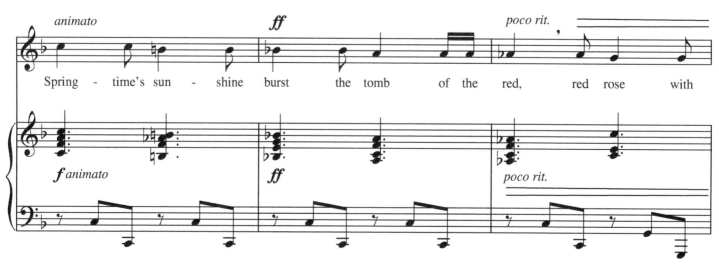

sweet per - fume? Will the long - lost love of the white rose bloom? Sing

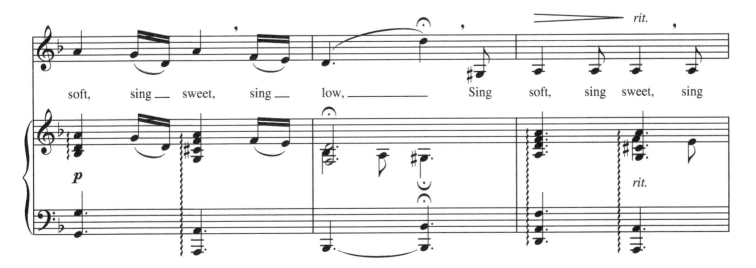

soft, sing — sweet, sing — low, Sing soft, sing sweet, sing

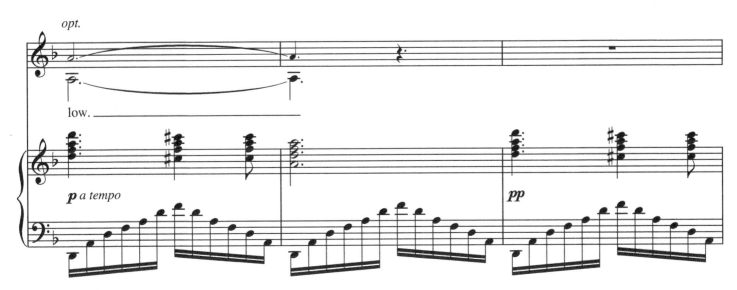

low.

TEARS

English words by
Charles Fonteyn Manney

Pyotr Il'yich Tchaikovsky

Fall in tor - rents, O tears! _____ O tears! _____

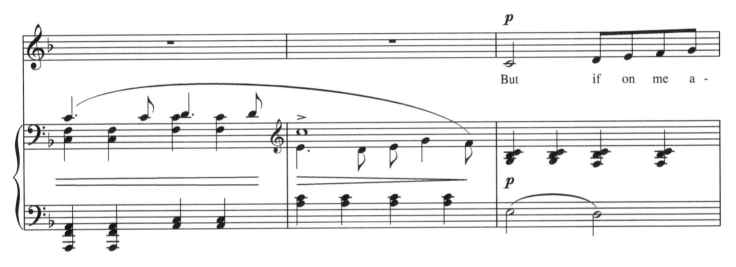

But if on me a -

gain new tor - ment you are heap - ing, If to a heart on

fire you add tor - tur - ing fears, _____ In pit - y cease to

72

73

for-bear, and leave my soul to die _____ by an - guish

shak - en! Fall not, O burn - ing tears, _____ O burn - ing tears! _____

No! No! Fall not, O tears!

UNDER THE GREENWOOD TREE

William Shakespeare

Arturo Buzzi-Peccia

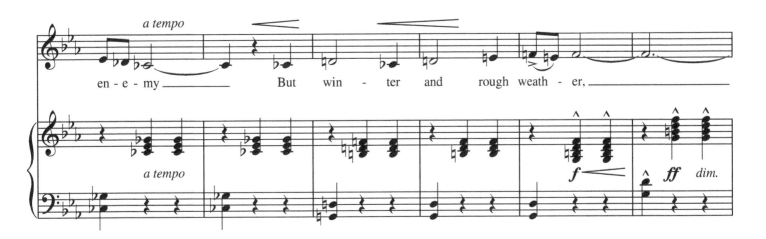

76

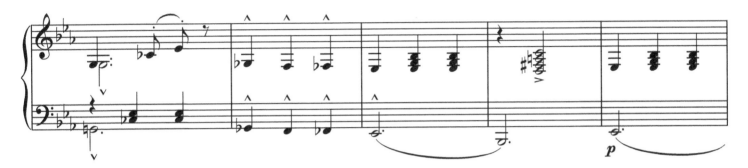

Tempo I

Who doth _ am - bi - tion _____ shun _____

And loves to live i' the sun, _____

Seek - ing __ the __ food he __ eats, __

p

rit.

And pleased with what __ he gets, __

rit.

dolce (avec charme) sostenuto

Come __ hith - er, come __ hith - er:

cantando

ben marcato

avec charme

Here shall he see No en - e - my. __ Oh, __

cresc.

staccato

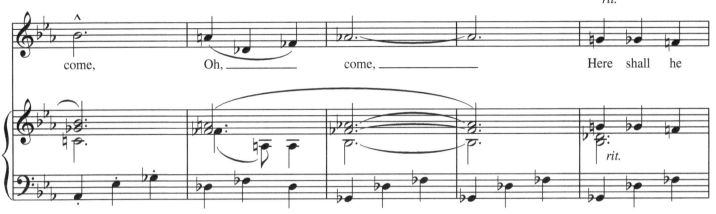

come, Oh, _____ come, _____ Here shall he

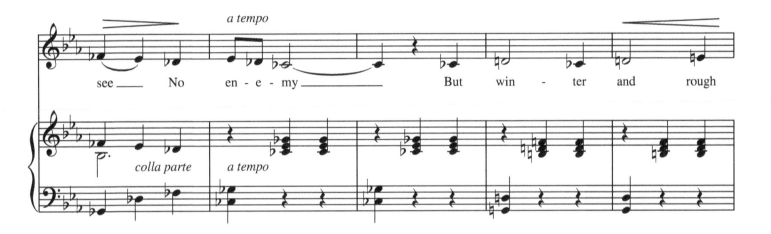

see ___ No en-e-my _____ But win - ter and rough

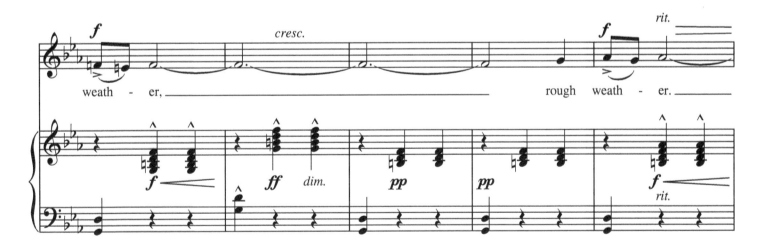

weath - er, _____ rough weath - er. _____

La, _____ la, _____

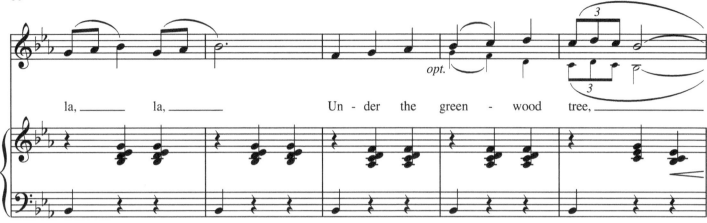

la, _____ la, _____ Un - der the green - wood tree, _____

La, _____ la, _____ la, la, la, _____ la, _____ la, la,

scherzando brillante

la, _____ la. _____

f

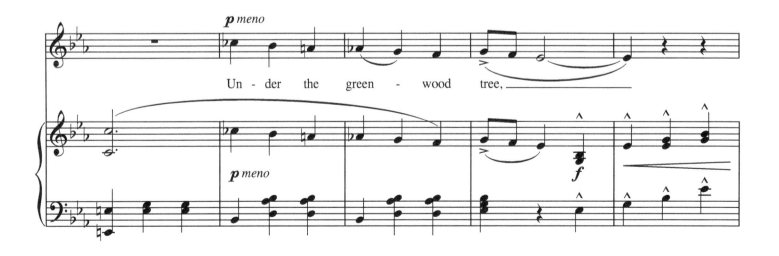

p meno

Un - der the green - wood tree, _____

p meno

f

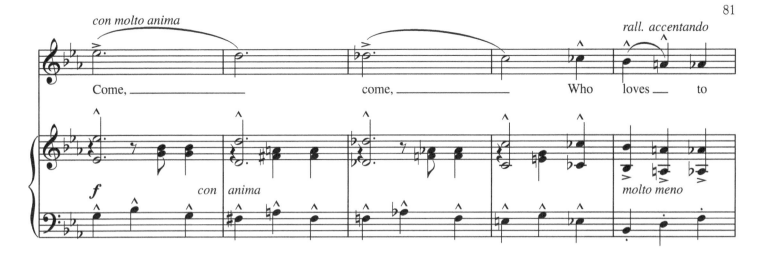
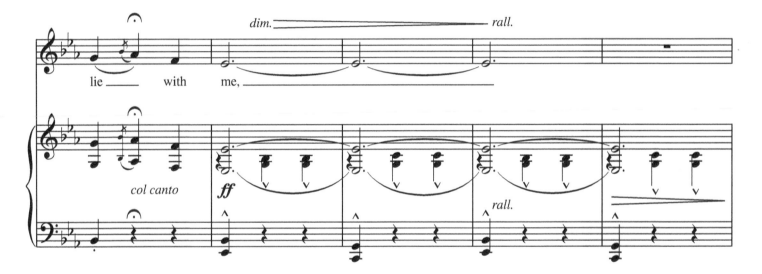
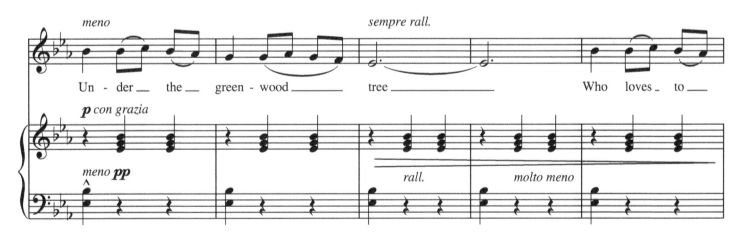
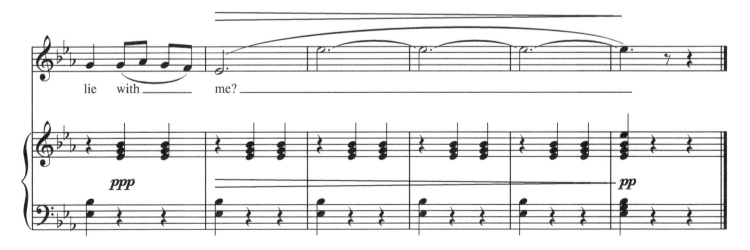

THE VALLEY OF LAUGHTER

Fred G. Bowles

Wilfred Sanderson

I know a val - ley sweet and __ gold - en, I know a val - ley fair to see,

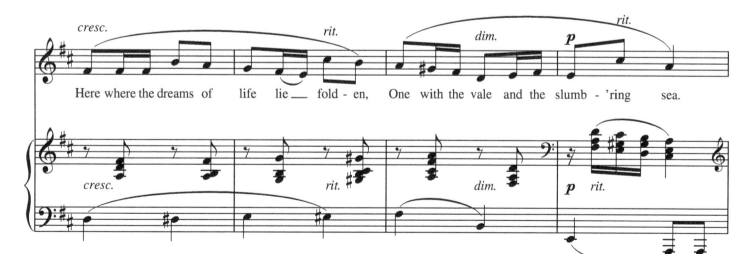

Here where the dreams of life lie __ fold - en, One with the vale and the slumb - 'ring sea.

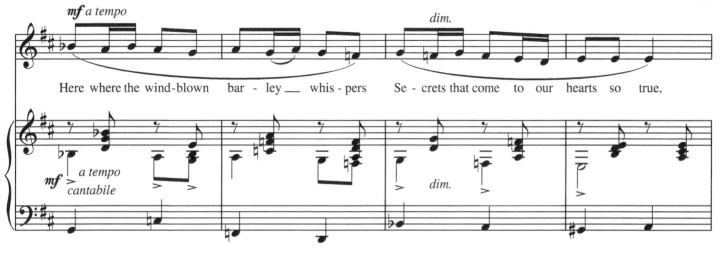

Here where the wind-blown bar - ley __ whis - pers Se - crets that come to our hearts so true,

Sun - light and shad - ow soft - ly __ tell me, Here 'twas you loved me and I loved

you, __ I loved you. __

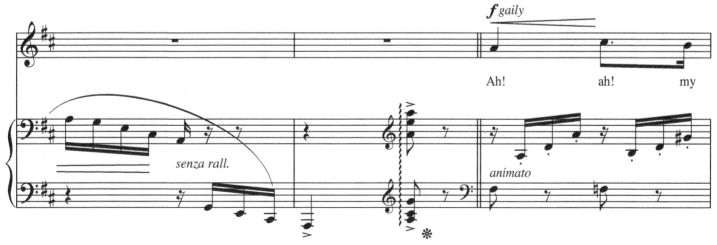

Ah! ah! my

laugh - ing __ val - ley, Winds blow as sweet to - day,

Here let us meet, here let us greet, One with the winds at play.

Skies are blue and rich the __ clo - ver, Laugh - ter rings the wide world __ o - ver;

Come a - way! _____ Come to - day! _____ Come and keep __ love's __ hol - i -

day. Come a - way! _____ Come to - day! _____ Come a - way! _____

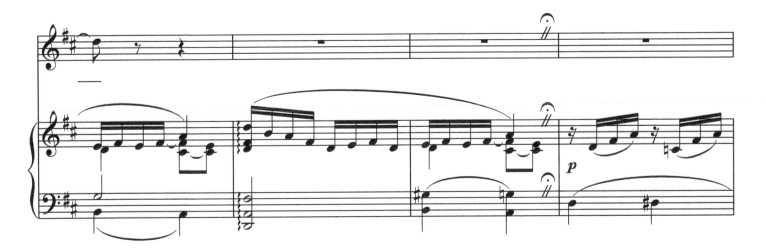

I know a val - ley sweet and _ gold - en, Lit by the light of the

har - vest moon; Sum - mer may pass and its dreams grow _ old - en, Fra - grant for ev - er our

Ah!   ah!   my laugh - ing ___ val - ley,   Winds blow as sweet to -

day,   Here let us meet,   here let us greet,

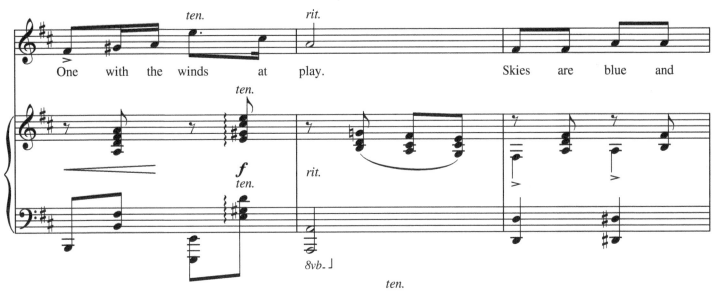

One with the winds   at   play.   Skies   are   blue   and

rich   the ___ clo - ver,   Laugh - ter rings   the   wide   world ___ o - ver;

* If not performing the cadenza, proceed to "come away!"

THE WINDS ARE CALLING
(Autumn)

Harold Simpson

Landon Ronald

quick - ly _____ you and I, _____

Good - bye! _____

poco rit.

p

a tempo

p

If aught that I have told you Should bring a mo-ment's

pain, Love, I will take and hold you With - in my arms a - gain; _____

p

both Pedals

WITHOUT THEE!

English words by
Paul England

Charles Gounod

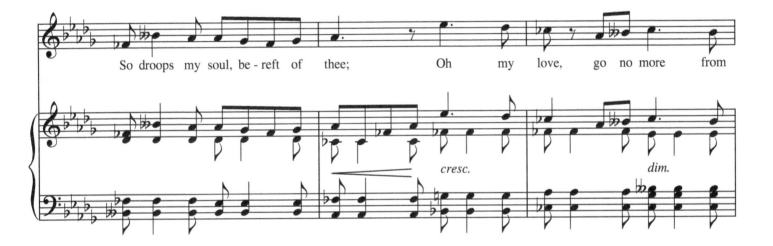

Like some poor bird whom day-light calls.___ To soar with song to heaven's do - min -

ion, E'en as he flies, wound - ed he falls, Mourn - ing a -

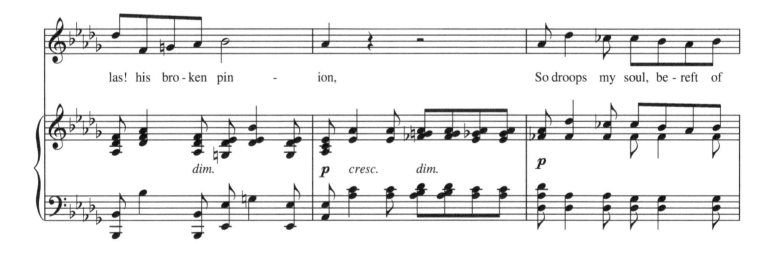

las! his bro - ken pin - ion, So droops my soul, be - reft of

thee, So droops my soul, be - reft of thee; Oh my

love, go no more from me! Oh my love, go no more from

dim. *p* *colla voce*

me!

a tempo *cresc.* *dim.*

Borne on a dark and an - gry tide, ___ With wind and

p

wave in fierce com - mo - tion, Some lone - ly bark, no hand to

guide,　　Aim - less - ly　drifts up - on the　o - 　cean,

So drifts　my soul, be - reft of　thee,　　So drifts　my soul, be - reft of

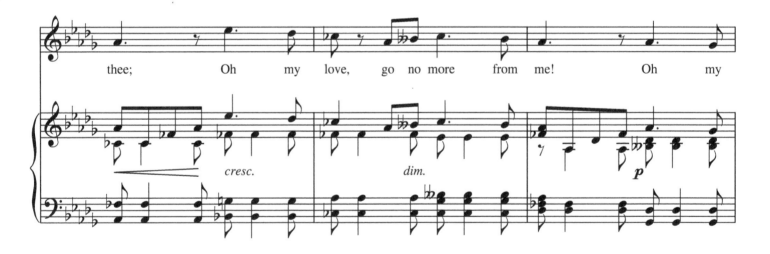

thee;　Oh　my　love,　go no more　from　me!　　Oh　my

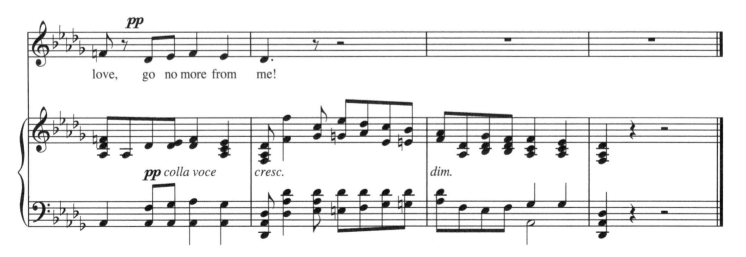

love,　go no more from　me!